Pegasus

A collection of short stories and poems

Suchandrima Ghosal

PAPER TOWNS
PUBLISHERS

First Published by
Paper Towns Publishers
72, Vishwanath Dham Colony,
Niwaru Road, Jhotwara,
Jaipur, 302012

Pegasus

ISBN Print Book - 978-93-6185-788-1

Printed in India

Acknowledgement

I wish to express my deepest gratitude to my family—Mom, Dad, Sister and Granny—whose unwavering love has been the cornerstone of this journey. My mother, Jaya Ghosal, has always been my first reader and a perceptive critic, providing invaluable guidance along the way. My father, Biswarup Ghosal, has provided steadfast encouragement in this endeavor and my sister, Meghna Ghosal, has inspired me to explore my creativity and reach for new heights. My Grandmother, Manisha Banerjee has infused me with her resolute determination and strength. I am profoundly thankful for their indomitable presence throughout this quest.

I would also like to extend my sincere appreciation to the editor of this book and my dear friend, Sounak Sarkar. His expertise and meticulous attention to detail have been instrumental in shaping this work, and I am deeply grateful for his support.

Content

Content

Childhood

Though I was born in North Kolkata, my ancestral home in the south of the city was my weekend hangout. My uncles, aunts and cousins lived there and not to forget my dear old grandmother, a rather amusing lady. I still picture her in her loose long gowns over her soft and supple skin weathered by time; I especially remember those summer afternoons, when her firm hands prepared the intoxicating pulp of wood apples mush. Frenzied by the whiff, we used to gather round her with cupped hands for her trademarked delicacy.

Her other source of attraction was tamarind-mixed rice. A pinch of kaffir-lime and salt, and the aroma was enough to soothe our cultivated ravenous appetites. As a little girl of six, it tantalized my senses, and I tried catching every nuance of the mouthwatering scent that promised a feast for my taste buds. Granny's traditional mixes and pulps were something that we always looked forward to. Our pentad, consisting of my sibling and three other cousins, was always on the lookout for secret jars of pickles and tamarind paste made especially by her. We played Sherlock Holmes, indeed, very seriously.

It is quite strange to fathom how innocent minds were back then; when quests were simpler and rewards more fulfilling; how Grandma's old-fashioned, exquisite dishes were more scrumptious than the modern day junk food. Maybe it wasn't the grub but the emotions that connected us, the passions that enchanted our hearts and made our childhood magical. But I think....... it was actually the taste of innocence unwrapped in front of us!

I have lived many lives

I have lived many lives;
Somewhere in your imagination I
have sustained myself;
Allowing myself to be smothered by
the caress of fantasy...
Living a vivid dream, days unfolded;

I have lived many lives;
On the beaches admiring the
sunset;
Let myself immerse and lose thy
oneself a little;
Remnants of my emotions peeking
around;

I have lived many lives;
In stories unraveled and unspoken
of;
In characters' sorrow and
unspoken sentiments;
Subtle yet naked to the
unconcerned eye;

I have lived many lives;
You can find bits and pieces of me –
in a child's laughter, in an obscure
piano note;
You will find more of me in ethereal
objects and
Less of me in me;

I have lived many lives;
Losing myself on the way;
The voidness that you can't fathom;
that you see;
Has their bills going to a different
address;
That's far away from me!

Aam

There was this enormous mango tree in the patch behind our house. It belonged to our neighbors', however that didn't stop the entire locality from reaping its benefits. I guess, they were accustomed to this truth and didn't mind it, mainly because the tree was like our Mother capable of feeding everyone in our neighborhood.

The tree was one of my favorite reasons why I waited all year for the summer season. The mango pulp squeezed from the offspring of the tree could definitely defeat the carbonated drinks at the market. We savored it on scorching summer afternoons.

During the monsoon, the beauty of the tree was like a treat to our eyes. Through the backdrop of the grey, cloud-filled sky, the green lushes swaying to extreme ends gave me an ecstatic joy. I used to spend hours admiring the child-like fervor infused in the tree's soul, its magical dance of companionship with the torrential downpour.

However, things took a turn during the hit of Amphan, the massive storm that hit our state and left everything devastated. We all had bolted our windows and gone to sleep the previous night. The next morning we woke up to our utter disbelief and saw our favorite Mangifera indica twisted and snapped; lying on the field like a shattered dream. The eerie noise of the storm was so overpowering that we failed to hear the tormenting cries of the majestic tall, towering giant.

I was heartbroken, I had lost my silent friend to the weeping universe. I blankly stared at the workers as they bestowed mercy upon it and put it out of pain. Vestiges of the magnificence lay all around scattered and I realized, I only had the memories to clutch onto. With a poignant void in my heart, I bid goodbye, promising to treasure the remembrances forever.

The Goddess of Illusion

The sails are billowed out owing to the fervent gales;
I sit at the corner of the vessel - desolated,
A heavy weight upon my heart;
My driver – Charon – smiles at me longingly.

They lied when they argued about how peaceful this journey was;
They lied when they performed the rites to bid me adieu;
It was to provide them closure; and here I am dwelling in my own solitariness;
Decades of intertwined relationships and fabricated pleasures-
Was it just an illusion after all?

Why does my heart then pine for
futile love?
Why does my heart then not
embrace the tranquility of eternity?
Why am I unable to fathom the
sanctity of this journey?
Why do I still visualize the ropes that
tether me behind?

Charon explains me to dedicate
time as time is all I have;
The ocean of time is my only asset;
I move on, sighing;
To only see from the corner of my
eye;
Maya whispering "au revoir".

Hope?

It was a winter morning. The orphan, an eight year old girl, was seated in a chair, all tensed. Her head lowered, the reverberations of her heartbeat pounded in her ears. She was waiting for years, for a long time, for someone and the day has finally arrived.

She looked up at the new blow-in with keen interest. The newcomer's forehead bore the evidence of the arrival of the first wrinkles and their deeply sunken eyes were unfathomable. The smile attracted her although it was not broad. She realized that this new guest in her life has undergone similar torment and adversities. She felt united by sorrow.

Destined to be an orphan by God, she had accepted the bitter truth of her existence. Her hankering desires were fading out when suddenly she purchased a miracle from the Almighty, selling her tears.

This lady had the face of a mother. It was rough and it resembled the unfinished work of an artist, but the imperfections are what the girl's heart craved. A masterpiece yet to be fulfilled has the satisfaction of art left to be done without celebrating the death of the labor undergone.

The Hope out of Pandora's box whispered in her years. Holding her mother's hand, she went out on a new voyage pining for a union with another part of her soul yet to be one.

Invisibly Close?

I am tired, walking down the lengthy
road
I want to rest my head on your
shoulder,
But unable to locate you; yes you
are there standing in the oblivion.
But cannot fathom you,

A blurry vision-
Is it a dream that has broken down
into shackles of reality?
A reality, unfelt and untouched, yet,
triggers my heart.......
I want to feel you, get close to you

Yet you are the misty droplets on a
rainy day
Waiting to get washed away by my
tears, into the dark sky
And I keep lingering to your soul
that was never mine
A frantic hand in the air, I hold you

But those are the pieces of my false
realities that I clutch clumsily
Aware of your non-existence I love
you
I wait for your love, to be immersed
in the cool waters of your scent

The fickle imagination of my mind,
the trickery is my reward
The murky background gifting false
hopes
And living with it – the greatest
treasures
I walk along holding the invisible
you.........

Loadshedding

The reminiscences that I gather from peeking into the tapestry of my past belong to some evenings marked by power cuts. Although these interruptions occurred mostly during the scorching heat of the summer, my sister and I eagerly waited for it. A slightly cool breeze and the familiar darkness would welcome us to the world of mythology. Enraptured by Mother's voice, I would sink into euphoria with her. A candle from the drawer and a hand fan were all was required for the ambience – a flicker of miracle would change hours of mundane homework into an evening of idling away Mr. Time. This was our center of attraction – being evasive towards our boring books to lose ourselves in captivating narratives.

Listening to Mother's magical childhood – she, recollecting her memories from the unforgotten lanes of Kanchrapara, was another favorite pastime of ours. Whether it was Pandavas' victories or the little bookworm in her railway bungalow, I was at all times transfixed by her tales. There were no villainous smartphones and laptops to steal the limelight of the engrossing blackouts.

The stories would go on endlessly, knitting our imagination into bright dream catchers and pinning them onto our hearts. Resting my head on Mother's lap, I would stare out into the vast expanse of the night sky, watching the moon play peek-a-boo. I often wondered "Might this be what Heaven feels like? "

The Afternoon Time

I sit at my window staring out into
the landscape;
Into the afternoon sky;
Where the drained sunshine falls
upon my cold bed,
What is it that you do world?

Faraway cries of the fantasy,
Summon me towards the abstract;
I feel the invisible voices reaching
out to where I am;

The inseparable and unknown
bindings that are yet left to be
discovered
Makes your heart wonder;
As to what will populate your empty
mind;
The sun prepares to sleep
While the dusk blankets the city;

My conscious filled with the
mystifying tenderness,
The ambiguity of the aroma all
around,
The unascertained dreams
enchants the gloomy sky;
Dear afternoon, I am enthralled by
your obscurity.

Her Social Curse

Her red and white bangles clinked as she rolled the *chapatis* on the *chakki* in the dim light of the kitchen – an expression of her inner self. Her face bore a sullen expression of abandonment, her living body merely a prison of her youthful soul.

It was around eight and her husband would arrive soon. She quickened her pace so as not to be late for her daily errand – the only identity she lived for.

Her kitchen window opened out to her neighbour's where a similar middle-aged woman like her was completing her daily chores. When the latter appeared, they exchanged glances and shared a weary smile, burdened by life's predicaments.

Suddenly her eyes fell on the deep scars and bruises on her neighbour's arm. She immediately averted her gaze – allowing the latter to hide her known mysteries. A victim of male chauvinism, getting inflicted by domestic violence was the quotidian cycle of the next door soul. She had heard her brutal screams strangling her own voice in the process.

A small click at the door announced her husband's return. At once she felt lonelier, as the mirage of solace disappeared in her bleak, barren desert. Such was her life – shut up within the four gloomy walls, an existence almost forgotten.

Dinner was eaten in absolute silence, her heart break unheard by the emotional deaf. The stillness in the house threatened her body to unearth her soul, the silence piercing her ears. A dead relation with her snobbish husband was what life gifted her after all the fearful years of marriage. Her condition was worse than that of the mute, unable to express her opinions and dreams, dreams that she had nurtured since childhood.

The indifference in his eyes as to her existence mauled her. She recognized the agonizing invisible bruises inflicted by her heartless husband.

She heard the faint cries of the other woman and they mirrored her own unheard voice. Both of them were whacked with rods by their husbands, only the weapons hurled at her were undetectable by the society. She was also the tortured soul, yet unlike the other, there was no name for the crime inflicted on her.

The night deepens and so does her solitude. Her tears, a dried up ocean, awaited excavation by no one. Her lifeless body eagerly waits for the pure touch of the funeral fire, a holy touch that will set her unfettered from her desolating existence. Her unnerving sinew tormented her tattered soul, forcing her once again to lie beside her soul's murderer.

Unrequited Love

A stupid girl I was,
Prepared to consume all your
sorrows,
I was there, only if you looked at me
The unspoken night knows, I craved
for your soul
A wink, a look wasn't enough!

Twice a week I uplifted my
enthusiastic eager
Many a dream, many a building up
of lovely gaiety
All in vain,
I know not what was there that you
couldn't fathom,
My eyes? Deeply in love with you?

You frantically went searching for
hearts to own
Yet you couldn't discern mine....
I waited for that radiant rainbow
That comes after the gloomy
shower
I waited...

The secrets of my pillow
My untold stories...
Will always be unheard by you...
But my grey haired days await a
blush
To just think about you!

Sleeping Beauty

His face was as white as snow. He couldn't grasp the weight of those appalling words that hammered his soul, " I am sorry, we couldn't save the mother."

It was a wintry morning when his wife had walked into the grey confines of this hopeful place named hospital clutching onto the escalated happiness at his sleeves. A new member was supposed to arrive that day pouring the rays of sunshine into their lives. However, fate took its turn and hours of unending hope for happiness turned desolate, empty and bruised.

He imagined her in the pink floral dress she wore when he met her for the first time, the very meeting that had felt like eternity. Long black curls fell over her shoulder and those mystifying eyes captivated his soul. He knew his longing, a desire never felt before between the yellow pages of his shabby books. Indeed, a princess out of a fairy tale she was to him and he had nurtured an aspiration in his heart to live a fairy tale with her.

The cold body covered in a shroud, rendered him still. He thought about his lost home that would never find its way back, the very home where the prince charming was supposed to live forever with his beloved princess. A desperate and shattered soul stood up against its mortal body. He expressed his desire to die where he could again be reunited with his lady love.

As he pondered over the sweet, pale face that lay in eternal sleep, an unconscious shriek broke his reverie. He looked up to find the uninvited member placed on his lap, a truth almost forgotten by his exhausted brain. Those same mystifying eyes stared back at him, the breath of dependence and want of love. For the first time after daylight, a smile curled up his lips, only to dissolve into hysterics; an out pouring of temporary madness giving way to a sober clarity. He was now a king to another princess and he would have to be prepared for a new kingdom, new promises, and a new fairy tale. He kissed his sleeping beauty goodbye and asked her to be asleep for a few more years to come. Someday, her prince charming would arrive, blowing out the spell of death and rescuing her from this deep sleep; to live happily ever after again. A fairy tale yet to be finished, after death.

The Blues of My Heart

You know you were not right that day,
When you apprehended your audacity to break my love
That I had caressed all these years

You know you were not right that day,
When you demanded to perforate my little dreams
The dreams that was all I held onto

You know you were not right that day,
When you pondered upon the thought
That I was just a timid goat-submissive

You know you were not right that day,
When you falsely manipulated your eyes
To prove something that was not to be proven

I know I was not right that day,
When I failed to realize
My tears were unfathomable
by you

I know I was not right that day,
When I demeaned myself
For my transcending love
towards you

I know I was not right that day,
When I trusted you
Unable to see your dark face
concealed by your mask

I know I was not right that day,
When I was stupid enough
To sell myself into the depths
of saudade

I know I am right today,
When I see the glittering fake
in your eyes
And stifle a smile

I know I am right today,
When I heal my wounded
dreams
With broken pieces of my
heart

I know I am right today,
When I make myself realize
That I have to wake my
deceased body

I know I am absolutely right today,
When I heroically battle my
emotions
To victory, to the goal I have
always awaited for.

My Murshidabad Trip

Our Murshidabad trip was a sudden plan decided on a whim one evening over cups of coffee and puffed rice. True to our decision, Father bought four tickets and bidding goodbye to the Goddess, we boarded the train on the eleventh day of the Pujas.

Scrambling into the coaches to secure our seat, my spirits soared to another level and my heart thumped in sync with the rhythmic vibrations of joy coursing through me. The first two hours of the train were quite interesting as I munched ravenously on *parathas* and egg curry enjoying the scenery outside. The food was undeniably delicious, evident from the envious expressions of nearby passengers who didn't get a taste. However, as time passed, the monotonous view of endless trees and fields lulled me into boredom. I dozed off in spite of the rattling sound of wheels and slept like a panda.

Suddenly there was a jerk and the train came to a halt. The engines hissed and the brakes squeaked. Startled and awake, I looked out the window and realized we had stopped at a station—Plassey. My heart skipped a beat. Although the yellowed pages of my history book had never truly captivated me, still a shiver ran down my spine when I realized the famous battle fought two centuries ago.

After a tiring journey of five hours, we arrived at our destination. We disembarked and walked a short distance to hire a *toto*. Taking rest for a while we immediately set out on our adventurous errand of reaping the historical past. Our first stop was The Hazarduari Palace, the centre of attraction of the place.

The Palace was a treasure trove of historical artifacts, swords crafted from ivory, pistols, spears, shields and many other things. I was greatly amused by the length of the rifles - some were even taller than me! The highly decorated palanquins, howdahs and sedan-chairs were mesmerizing. Certain items stood out: a bowl that changed colour when exposed to poison, ornamental cutlery and stunning oil paintings. The founder of the Palace, Humayun Jah - a strikingly handsome man with intellectual, gleaming eyes, humorously piqued my interest!

After exploring the Palace, we boarded a tonga and my happiness reached new heights. The journey continued with visits to other fascinating landmarks: the houses of Jagath Seth, Daku Devi Singh and the Durbar Hall of the Nawab. The room where prisoners were hanged down an iron chain, sent a chill shiver through my spine as I imagined myself a witness to the scene. Sarees made of gold threads and muslin, and the antique furniture revealed their true luxury life.

The tonga ride was the cherry on top to our excursion. The constant melodious sound of the horse's hooves between the green landscapes enveloped me with a warm aroma. The lush trees swirled and swayed covering the sunset - orange and apple red, a perfect setting to soothe the human mind. The driver, a cheerful and spirited man, also added mirth to our heart brimming setback.

It was almost evening when our journey came to a halt. Although exhausted, the gleam in our eyes reflected the fullness of our hearts. Murshidabad was more than a destination—it was a place where we connected our spirits with the past, created countless memories, and tuned our emotions to the harmonious strings of vibrant history.

Love

You touch my hand;
A warmly gesture of your pure soul
The aroma of you fills me,
Uplifts me;
An ecstatic joy
Your moistened lips on my trembling ones

You captivate my soul
Enamored of you
I feel your protection around me,
Your soft strokes on my body
Helps me to sink in your love
You Hypnotize me;

Your caressing of my tresses
Titillate my senses;
Under the dark, chilly night
I burn within the heat in you....
You sanctify my soul
Oh Dear!
With your passionate love!

The Bhasan

He hastened to put on his hand-me-down shirt and pants. Even though, they were cast-offs, for him it was brand new. He carefully parted his hair at the side and smiled at his accomplishment. He was finally ready. Descending the tenebrous spiral staircase of the old orphanage that he called home, he joined his inmates with a lifted spirit. It was *Dashami* and as promised they would visit the holy *ghats* of the Ganges to bid farewell to the Goddess. He was exuberant, eager to see the Mother one last time, his only mother, apart from the absence in his bleak, barren life.

The jamboree at the *ghat* was overwhelming for the tattered souls draped in palls. Their administrator kept a close watch and prevented them from drifting away, however the shindig somehow managed to meander their joyful minds. Workers chanted "*Bolō Dugga Mayī kī Jai*" before flipping the mammoth-sized idols into the pious waters. He looked at the Mother's face enchantingly as if he could personify the lifeless block as one of her own.

He had long craved a mother with a warm face and hands filled with love, similar to those of the manufactured statues. He found himself relaxed, pouring into the Goddess' eyes and longed for those faux hands reach out to adore and caress him. For years, he had been pining for a loved soul within the unrewarding walls of his abode. Yet another year, he sacrifices and farewells the Mother into the unknown.

One final morning he finally gets his *Daak*, a calling out he had been waiting for, dreaming and fabricating castles in the air. Will the Goddess allow him to dwell in her own? He went up encouragingly to meet her. It was the same face, a mother's face, just as he had witnessed in the towering blocks of hope in the godly pandals. It was time, time for his *Bhasan* along with his deity, towards his Home.

Maturity

How do you know that you have
matured?
Is it when you stop playing with dolls
and remote cars?
Or is it when you have tons of
syllabus to complete?
Or is it when the unspoken feelings
dig their graves inside the heart -
unfathomable by the world?

The warm touch of your parents-
a patron in your deserted hotel, a
feeling of warmth in all the
loneliness.
When you suddenly start
embracing cold behavior with all
your might,
Alas! It's charring your heart –

You frantically search hitherto for
love,
for trust;
Desolation vibrated.
The world looks like a thick thorny
bush
And you are unsuccessful in finding
roses,
Roses that are red and beautiful.

You know you are out of your
prince charming ideas
Preparing yourself for the battle
that is approaching you.
A craving heart pining desperately
for a trusted soul,
A soul that would connect you to
eternity.

You are a murderer,
You kill and lash yourself every day,
By the millions of brains outside
you,
Not knowing one is enough to heal
you,
Not realizing that, that one is you.

You sit by the river pondering why
you are so different from the world,
Different from everyone
And then you are suddenly
attracted by a small sapling –
That is so unique, so unlike, yet so
beautiful;

You find your true self but are
unable to decipher it;
you don't try; keeping aside for
someone else?
The tears in your eyes have long
been forgotten;
You only remember the heavy
feeling that you have in your heart.
This world, so obsessed by itself,
You realize you have matured.

5 Minutes

My usual journeys to University used to involve two buses. Although the reconstruction of the Tala Bridge incentivized me to excavate a new world filled with mystery and wonder.

I started travelling by train about a month ago. My local train journeys have now become a part of my daily routine. When I commenced such a new adventure, my heart was filled to the brim with excitement to capture this new magnificence.

The turmoil of boarding the train is devastating- extreme forces are exerted as people push others out of the way for an invisible and unreasonable race. In spite of such adversities, my level of happiness stays the same - the credit entirely goes to the following part of my joyful journey.

I usually stand at the doorway to feel the gusting wind across my face. The faraway cries of hawkers slowly come closer and enchants my heart. The contented look on their faces when they succeed in selling their merchandise resembles a child's innocence.

Salted *badams* and peas, wooden combs, fried *chanachur* packets, cotton earbuds, fragmented perfumes, glossy earrings, juicy fruits, naphthalene balls and so many more heart- throbbing items are displayed before us. The mixed, extravagant colors make me feel like a child again.

The rhythmic motion of the jingling sound when the wheels kiss the track uplifts my soul to new heights. People, vehicles, trees, stray dogs fleetingly pass by, their temporary presence quickly erased. Such exalted levels of ecstatic joy captivate me and make me a prisoner of romanticism.

My heart breaks at the sight of the words "Dumdum Junction" painted on the tarnished walls. That marks the end of my childhood and with a heavy heart I walk towards the auto stand thriving on my adult life. However, 5 minutes or eternity?

A Lonely Soul

The night sky is starless,
A pitch-black curtain draped over
the universe;
Her moist eyes tried to pierce
through the darkness,
An unfinished novel and a tangled
pair of earphones lie beside her,

The colour slowly fades away from
her heart,
She hears a hammer hitting hard-
Only to realize that the
The pounding comes from within.

Her naked bruised soul
Longs to be caressed;
But quiet!
Only the dark night knows her
deepest secrets.

She is engulfed by the canopy of
blackness,
Where she keeps her fears locked
away,
Alas! The wind soothes down;
The cosmos becomes dumb.

The photo album etched in her heart,
Those beautiful memories......
With her exhausted smile,
She escapes the reality,
That stabs her with the dawn of the morning sun.

The Journey

She stopped at the tube well to fill up her empty bottle. The refreshing, cool waters soothed only her exhausted body; it couldn't touch her soul. She took a sip and continued on her tiring journey.

It might be noon by now as the sun was scorching right above her head. She sat huddled on the pavement to eat her lunch- a couple of stale chapatis with pickles, the only recreation in her overtiring work. After all, she was just a street vendor - how much freedom could God bestow upon her? This was the only time to dwell in the past, to fall into the luxury of grief and sorrow that had strangled her. She was twenty-five years old when her husband left her, shattering her dreams of romance and marriage. The responsibility of three children and an old mother was indeed enervating but being a coward would never help. Romance was now to her the shiny coins in her hand, the crispy sound of notes that bring food to her family- a sarcasm by the Almighty.

She stooped to pick up her basket to continue in her tedious errand. Today, there were ripe lemons. Sometimes she brought vegetables or hand-woven articles with her, articles that she makes at night by the light of the hurricane, the only witness to her diligence.

A flash of the faces of her children spiritualizes her with a new sense of sinew. She would now walk with greater strength and be a hero in the battlefield that is staged in her life. Her only victory is the happiness that she sees in her children when she returns home in the evening, that is what encourages her to perform her part well in her life's drama.

She stops here and there when passers-by ask for her lemons and then again continues her journey. A thin dark, gaunt woman haggard by the miseries of life! Was the Almighty blind enough not to notice her?

The sun was setting emitting its last crimson rays of light. It was time for her to return to her nest just like the birds.

Sitting at the edge of the compartment, the forceful wind beating against her face, she re-energizes herself. The speeding train resembles her life, heading forward leaving behind the dark silhouette of buildings and trees - beautiful yet insignificant in her life. Moving with its rhythm, she eagerly waits to reach her home, her ultimate destination.

Lost Childhood

In the dusky twilight,
With a book in my hand
Embracing the sun's departure
With the wind blowing on my face

And the trees' dance in the far
silhouette
The songs of the crickets;
Me, away in my faraway land
Where evil doesn't exist

And flowers fulfill you;
Me, Beaming with radiance;
The peeking moon through the cotton clouds
The symphony of frogs from the nearby pond

My heart throbbing with the tranquility
The presence of serenity both inside and outside of me;
That is long lost and forgotten;
Missing myself from my Childhood!

Shroud Of Her Sorrow

The gusting wind was hitting against the window panes and the misty droplets of the downpouring water trickled down the glass. She did not watch how those two drops raced against each other. She was busy remembering someone. Someone who was far away from her warm hugs and kisses. The dark, lonely apartment was only a bleak shadow of her own consciousness; the consciousness that did not contain any glimpses of reality. He was her conscience, the feeling she enwrapped herself with.

She felt cold and gathered the blanket around her body tighter yet the wind penetrated her heart. Soon, she realized, it would drill a hole there. But someone was colder, in the icy graves, someone who did not have a blanket. She couldn't be selfish enough to think only about herself.

The tender raindrops on her lips where he touched his own, when their bodies met and united, lit a fire in her heart. He always shielded her from the brutal wind, enveloping her with the warm blanket of his love. She craved that special serape to enfold her from the savage hostilities of nature; a shroud?

She relieves his ripples of laughter, his enchanting smell, his sliding head in the pillow and rejuvenates herself again. The pattering rain drops - a lullaby and she rocked herself to sleep.

Phoenix

In the dark, murky background,
He lays with his face stooped down;
Weary upon the world,
His mind; a burnt pyre that lay
across his side;

The heap of ashes surround him;
Soothe and gulp him down;
Somewhere thy remains the ember
smoldering-
Pulsing gently.........

It evokes a glare and then a spark;
His mind being the incendiary-
Out from the ashes, it ascends,
Majestic and royal it stands....

Burdens on his shoulders;
And a broken brain....
Resilience to adversity; it rises....
Phoenix in human form?

My Boyhood Years

When I remember my boyhood years, I often think about my joyous days when I had meaningful relationships with my brothers – all those prankish ideas that we dutifully executed over the days. I remember my adolescence striding over towering walls that covered the boundaries of our two-storeyed house and climbing the thick trunks of the jackfruit tree – with my younger brother who was my constant partner in crime. Often at these times, Father would return home with a stern face and we would immediately sit with flipped books and chanting voices straining all through the house.

During power cuts, we used to huddle around the hurricane light and pretend to study hard with dedication. We would patiently wait for someone to fall asleep and when one finally would, we used to come out with our cunning tricks. Sometimes we placed dead mosquitoes on their cheeks just to slap them hard again. However, I was intelligent enough to not become the victim.

School was amusing too. We gathered early to fish in the pond situated behind the old building. We made fishing rods out of old brooms, plastic bottles and iron wire that acted as the hook. We used to secretly pocket crumbs of bread during breakfast and use them as bait. The fish wasn't the source of attraction though - the amusement of breaking rules definitely had the upper hand.

One incident I particularly remember – I was there on the top of the jamun tree at my school; my hands cupped with its delicious offspring and me devouring them with great relish, when our headmaster strolled in. The other boys ran away in fear and I was stuck there for an hour with the headmaster glaring at me and promising me a long list of punishments he would endow me with. However, being the top student in the class, I was mildly spared later on.

Often I reminisce about the times during Vishwakarma Puja, when we scattered around looking for broken light bulbs and other abrasive materials to sharpen the strings of our kites. Our bleeding fingers and uplifted spirits, as we screamed *Bho Katta*, created a roaring sensation across the *paras*. The azure sky painted with the blotches of colorful kites were the rainbows in our lives in a world without internet.

There were no lavish meals on our plates frequently, or luxury apparel to die for, though we painted our life's canvas with the brightest colors of our innocence and youth. The house was our abode and not a mark of property; and festivities were fun, not a show of competitive extravagance. With loads of money in our pockets and inside our spacious flats, I can still hear the screams around our neighborhood, *Bho Katta!*

Intoxicated

Amidst the cozy and tranquil light;
In the soft corner of the sofa,
I sit staring at you....
Feeding on your love for my
ravenous appetite...

How I have longed for this
moment....
How have I longed to dive into your
madness...
To have my soul join in the
craziness
Of loving you; Of admiring you;
Everyday!

Never have I been inebriated by an
old bottle of wine;
Never have I been rapturous over
smoke,
But you did magically engulf me in
your heart;
Welcomed me as I surrendered to
your intoxicating essence;

You are the wine that I want to
submerge in;
The smoke that sedates my senses;
Your presence is the only drug I
desire......
I am the pirate who dwells in your
ocean of love!

The Orphan

The blazing furnace lit up the western sky and the monstrous flames had already started engulfing the derelict building. There were loud screams everywhere of fear and anxiety that disturbed the softness of the atmosphere. The neighbours had already immersed themselves in their idea of help and the fire brigade would arrive soon.

A fourteen year old survivor sat huddled beside the post box. She did not have a single drop of tear nor any lingering fear in her eyes. She admired the incandescent flames adorned with the bright colours of orange and red - the divine heartless beauty separating the loved ones. As the thick grey smoke billowed into the sky, she remembered her mother's fear-stricken face when she was handed down from her parent's warmth to a cold stranger. The setting was the same, yet a different story. She had cried that day. The agonizing shrieks of her family had induced her to pour out her hot, brimming tears into the world that welcomed departed souls with misery. Eleven she was when she witnessed the dead corpses of her parents and brother – laid down in front of her, a failure in the battle with destiny. The giant conflagration had ravenously gobbled her pieces of happiness providing in return a hollow heart.

The arrival of the fire-brigade with its loud music broke her thoughts. She attentively noticed their swift and stern attitude towards their work. Immediately they led out hose pipes to calm down the world's fiercest giant from charring the orphanage, the only home of the protagonist. The copious black smoke choked her and she was pulled to another place – a hand which carried the tinge of her mother's warmth. She remembered her mother's rough hands that appeared so soft to her, when she caressed her hair – the smell of jasmine oil under the sultry breezy afternoon sky. The tingling voice of her mother was a melody her ears had long forgotten. The jokes of her father and brother at dinner coupled with fresh chapatis gradually faded away and escaped from the face of the world, only scattered fragments left in her heart. They were poor, her father only a mason and mother a homemaker but still they churned happiness out of such meagre ingredients. Such was her life that even the Almighty envied it. She stifled a laugh at the designed mockery flung at her.

Slowly and gradually, the inhabitants of the orphanage were rescued. She waited for no one as none was her friend. The vibrant colours of the villainous flames had died down as the sun crept below the horizon.

Her heart was heavy – the loving memories were its cause. It was too unbearable for her. The ornaments that adorned her heart pained her – beauty with its curse. One day she might have the courage to throw them down just to feel lighter and painless – death or a dim hope like a faint flickering light in the darkest sky! Three years had made her strong, matured, independent of handling her own sorrows where she was afraid of none, not even of the turbulent flames that had surrounded her. She looked around. The fire had left a gloomy scene and the dense smog polluted the atmosphere like a black cat creeping around the streets. She looked up and in the faint smoke, she recognized three beautiful faces – faces of her family smiling at her, at her bravery in this heartless world.

Into The Mind Of A Vile Woman

I sit at the corner of the bed
A twitching smile on my lips
To please your hankering soul, O
Man!
I am ready to satisfy your yearning
desire.

You come to me
Under this very night, under the
holy shining stars
A heart not filled with love, or
sympathy
But only a lecherous gaze to touch
my bosom.

You are not a disgrace to yourself
Not an ignominy to the society,
But I am pelted with its stones, pebbles
My fault? Just to feed you with my own?

I prevent thousands of molestation everyday
Yet I am worshipped by none
A devil in human form I am
And you a God, in your foul form?

Money truly speaks happiness
Cuz its money that makes her the
Deity
Whereas I in my poor, wretched
state
Is untouchable by the community.

The dawn is approaching dear
Hurry to your wife that waits for
you,
You have a life of your own unlike
this lifeless block
That embraces the night to hide
away her sorrows!

The Grey Autumn

The arrival of dusk made the street look like an old photograph, everything having a tinge of grey. The color was reflected into the pounding heart of the greyed man. The dwindling day-light forced the chirping birds to retreat to their nests which was a signal for him. He got up from his creaking bamboo chair and placed the unfinished Rabindra Rachanabali in the dusty rack. It was time for *adda*. A tuscan sun colored kurta and similar pyjamas adorned him greatly. It was 2018 unlike his father's era of holding the *dhuti's kocha* for a stroll outdoors.

That was a time for flamboyant Bengali culture, where the educated middle class was exclusively concerned with establishing their traditional ethics - from chanting poetries of Tagore to relishing in the works of Ray and Bankim Chandra- most of them being obsolete nowadays.

A few drops of *attar* perfume perfected his attire and taking his wooden walking stick, he descended down the streets.

The shadowed environment failed to soften the thumping heart of the seventy-five-year-old man. This was the time where he would feel himself, fondle his identity and relieve his childhood. His busy family loved him but the solitude in his heart felt like a searing pain – the *adda* engulfing some of his sorrows. It was a temporary relief for him. He would be rejuvenated again, alive for another time after his wife's death.

His mind drifted along his childhood memories. Maybe today he would talk about his football matches in the rain fed mud while the booming *shanks* were blown to soothe Indra's anger. Or maybe he would discuss the literary differences between Shakespeare and Tagore; truly a knowledgeable reader was what the group wanted.

The grey sky deepened into a misty black, darkening his surroundings. With scurried steps he raced towards the chair-drawn courtyard, unlike the traditional *royak*, like a little boy yet to live life all over again.

Calling out!

In the stillness of the moonlight sky;
The wind soothes down and
whispers;
Among the rustling, playful sprouts;
That tethers your soul to theirs;

The cresting, roaring ocean waves;
That sing a melodious siren song,
The rhythmic waves that dance
about;
Capture your essence; baffles you;

The howling spirits of the night;
The faraway cries from the woods,
Will bind your mind in a mystifying essence;
And engulf you into a warm embrace....

Through wide valleys and tall mountains;
Where echoes ride through air,
The fluttering woodpecker summons you
Into the enthralling twilight;
A lost pathway into resonance.......

About the Author

Suchandrima Ghosal

Suchandrima was a bookworm from a young age, spending countless afternoons immersed in the worlds crafted by Christie, Ray, and Bond. Each story transported her to thrilling landscapes and intricate mysteries, sparking her own dreams of becoming a writer. Yet, as life unfolded, her path diverged from that dream.

Instead, she found joy in teaching English to students in her home, sharing her love for literature with eager minds. Amidst the hustle of lessons and daily corporate life, Suchandrima carved out time to weave narratives, exploring a tapestry of emotions, both joyful and sorrowful. In these pages, she invites readers into a realm where dreams intertwine with reality, offering a glimpse into her creative spirit and the stories that have shaped her heart, including the poignant tales that echo her deepest reflections.